Mast

Rigging

ing top

Gunshot holes

Cannons

Gun crews

Lower gun
deck

The story of

Doomed Ships

Shipwrecks Ghost Ships and Abandoned Vessels

Penny Clarke

BOOK HOUSE

1 3 5 7 9 8 6 4 2

Published in Great Britain in 2008 by
Book House, an imprint of
The Salariya Book Company Ltd
25 Marlborough Place, Brighton BN1 1UB
www.salariya.com
www.book-house.co.uk

A CIP catalogue record for this book is available
from the British Library.

Printed and bound in China.

Author: Penny Clarke
Illustrators: David Antram
Mark Bergin
Bill Donohoe
Nick Hewetson
John James
Tony Townsend
Hans Wiborg-Jenssen
Gerald Wood
Editor: Tanya Kant
Editorial Assistants: Mark Williams,
Rob Walker

Penny Clarke is an author and editor
specialising in children's information books.
She lives in Norfolk, England.

HB ISBN-13: 978-1-906370-00-8
PB ISBN-13: 978-1-906370-01-5

PAPER FROM
SUSTAINABLE
FORESTS

Visit our website at **www.salariya.com**
for **free** electronic versions of:
You Wouldn't Want to be an Egyptian Mummy!
You Wouldn't Want to be a Roman Gladiator!
Avoid Joining Shackleton's Polar Expedition!
Avoid Sailing on a 19th-Century Whaling Ship!

Contents

WHY WRECKS?

17th-century globe

WATCH ANY STORMY SEA, with waves pounding at seashores and flinging large rocks around like grains of rice, and you may wonder why so few ships are wrecked. Faced by the sea's power even the largest ships are fragile, so it's amazing that most complete their voyages safely. This book is about some of the ships that didn't. Terrible weather, terrible captains, mutinous crews and broken equipment are as disastrous for today's ships as they were for galley crews four thousand years ago. A container ship with engine failure is as helpless as a sailing ship with a smashed mast, and both are at the sea's mercy. But at least today's modern communications can bring rescue – something beyond the wildest dreams of early sailors.

Abandon ship!

A good captain goes down with his ship!

Good thing you're the captain then!

Trophy warships

War has caused more shipwrecks than storms have. Warships armed with guns first appeared in the 16th century. Making an enemy's ship sink was good, but destroying the sails and masts was better, because then the ship could be boarded and taken as a trophy.

The 'New' World

CHRISTOPHER COLUMBUS reached what is now called the West Indies in 1492. Other European explorers followed, discovering a 'new' continent with wealthy civilisations. The explorers were dazzled by what they saw – temples and palaces decorated with gold and silver. But the newcomers soon destroyed these civilisations, looting their treasures and taking them back to Europe, whose rulers had funded many of the voyages.

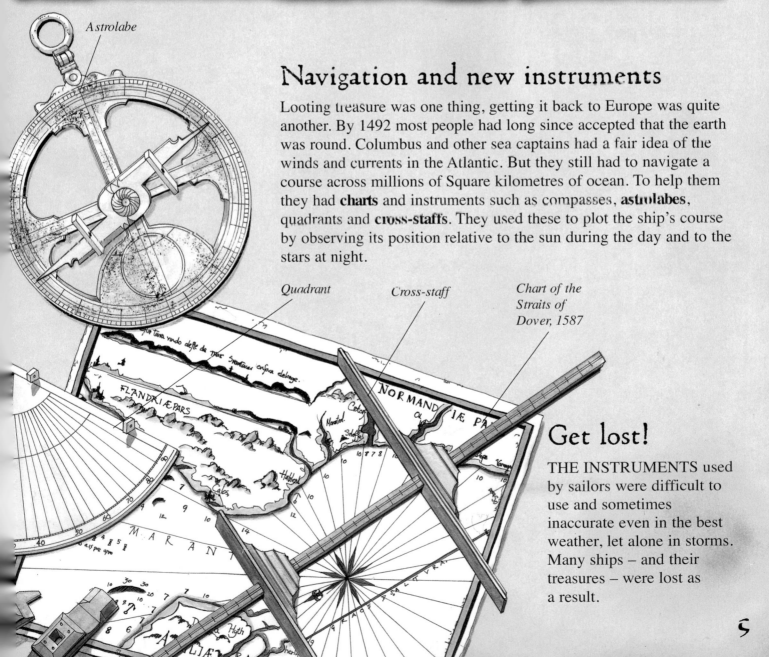

Astrolabe

Navigation and new instruments

Looting treasure was one thing, getting it back to Europe was quite another. By 1492 most people had long since accepted that the earth was round. Columbus and other sea captains had a fair idea of the winds and currents in the Atlantic. But they still had to navigate a course across millions of Square kilometres of ocean. To help them they had **charts** and instruments such as compasses, **astrolabes**, quadrants and **cross-staffs**. They used these to plot the ship's course by observing its position relative to the sun during the day and to the stars at night.

Quadrant

Cross-staff

Chart of the Straits of Dover, 1587

Get lost!

THE INSTRUMENTS used by sailors were difficult to use and sometimes inaccurate even in the best weather, let alone in storms. Many ships – and their treasures – were lost as a result.

ANCIENT WRECKS

Coin from an ancient Mediterranean shipwreck

WHEN WAS the first ever shipwreck? No-one knows, but archaeologists do know that ships were making voyages around the Mediterranean Sea at least 4,000 years ago. How do they know? From shipwrecks! The Mediterranean is a relatively calm sea, but sudden storms can still blow up. Around its shores rich civilisations developed, encouraging trade – and shipping – along its coasts.

ONE ROMAN SHIP sank off southern Italy between AD 200 and 250. Its cargo of black marble sarcophagi (stone coffins) probably came from Asia Minor (modern Turkey).

THIS BRACELET shows the size and wealth of the Roman Empire. The stones are from Africa and the gold from Britain or Spain.

THE GIGLIO SHIP with its cargo of musical instruments, pottery and at least one bronze helmet sank between 750 and 500 BC.

THE SCULPTURES of the wrecked Greek merchant ship Lysippos *are now in the Paul Getty Museum, USA.*

FOUND NEAR TUNIS in 1907, the Mahdia ship had a cargo of marble columns and statues when it sank.

ITALY

Mediterranean Sea

LIBYA

Roman galleys

First-century Roman galley

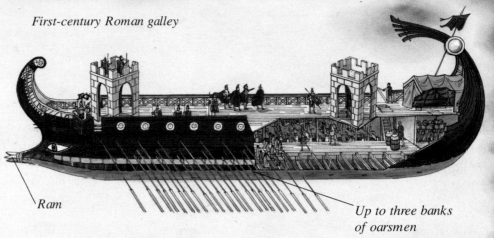

EARLY SHIPS in the Mediterranean were **galleys**, powered by rowing. Some had sails for steering and to provide extra speed when the wind blew from behind. The Roman galley (right) was a warship, with up to three banks of oarsmen on each side and an underwater ram at the **bow** which could damage enemy ships.

Ram

Up to three banks of oarsmen

Black Sea

THE CAPE ARTEMISIUM ship was lost to the sea for thousands of years, and found in 1927. A magnificent bronze statue (below, right) was recovered.

TURKEY

THE YASSI ADA ship and its cargo of tools, lamps and gold coins sank around AD 625.

GREECE

THIS BRONZE STATUE (below) represents either Poseidon, Greek god of the sea, or Zeus, king of the gods. It was found in the wreck of the Cape Artemisium ship and is now in the National Museum in Athens.

DATING FROM around AD 1000, the Serce Limani ship sank off Marmaris (in modern Turkey).

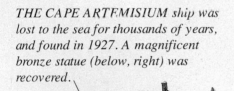

WRECKED ROMAN galley discovered in 1900 off southern Greece.

WRECKED around 1200 BC, this Phoenician ship carried bronze and copper.

EGYPT

ROMAN WRECKS

Roman merchant ship of about two thousand years ago.

TWO THOUSAND years ago, the Mediterranean Sea was busy with trading ships. Bad storms made it too dangerous to sail in winter, so trade was limited to spring and summertime. Even so, many ships were wrecked. But were storms the only cause? Bad seamanship and unseaworthy or overloaded ships also caused shipwrecks. Wrecks were disasters for everyone involved, but for the archaeologists who found them centuries later, these doomed ships have been a rich source of information. We have learnt far more about Roman ships and trade from shipwrecks than from any successful voyage!

High seas and higher risks!

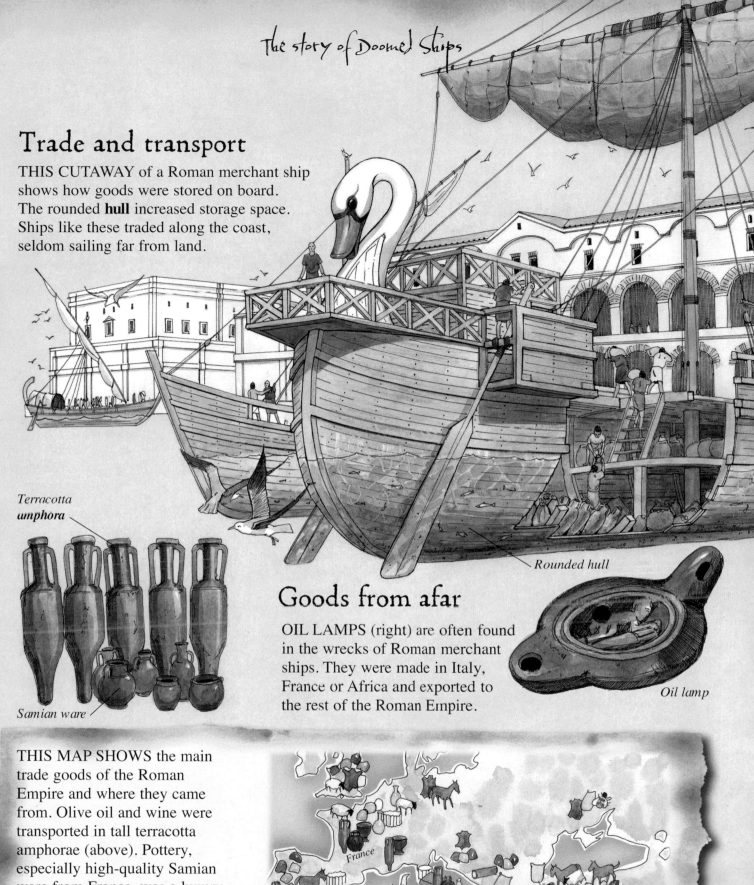

Trade and transport

THIS CUTAWAY of a Roman merchant ship shows how goods were stored on board. The rounded **hull** increased storage space. Ships like these traded along the coast, seldom sailing far from land.

Terracotta **umphora**

Samian ware

Rounded hull

Goods from afar

OIL LAMPS (right) are often found in the wrecks of Roman merchant ships. They were made in Italy, France or Africa and exported to the rest of the Roman Empire.

Oil lamp

THIS MAP SHOWS the main trade goods of the Roman Empire and where they came from. Olive oil and wine were transported in tall terracotta amphorae (above). Pottery, especially high-quality Samian ware from France, was a luxury item for wealthy citizens. The Romans also imported so many lions to fight gladiators that lions became extinct in North Africa and Syria.

France

Rome

North Africa

VIKING VOYAGES

GREENLAND

ARCHAEOLOGISTS ARE sure Viking seafarers reached North America a good four centuries before Columbus landed in the West Indies. Certainly the Vikings were excellent sailors, regularly ravaging the shores of north-western Europe. They even sailed up the Thames to attack London early in the 11th century. They were known as Norsemen or Normans because they came from the north. The area of France where they settled is still called Normandy. In 1066 Duke William, the son of one of these settlers, invaded Britain – the start of the Norman Conquest.

Prow of the Oseberg ship, around AD 800

THE STANGARFOLI ship was wrecked off Greenland in 1189.

THE OSEBERG SHIP, the burial place of a Viking woman, was discovered in 1903. It was buried in a mound which was airtight, preserving many objects in it.

A Viking tomb

SOME SURVIVING VIKING SHIPS were used to bury important people. The dead person was put on board with objects to help them in the next life. Then everything was covered with a mound of stones and earth.

Viking ships were explored by divers in Roskilde Fjord, Denmark, in 1957.

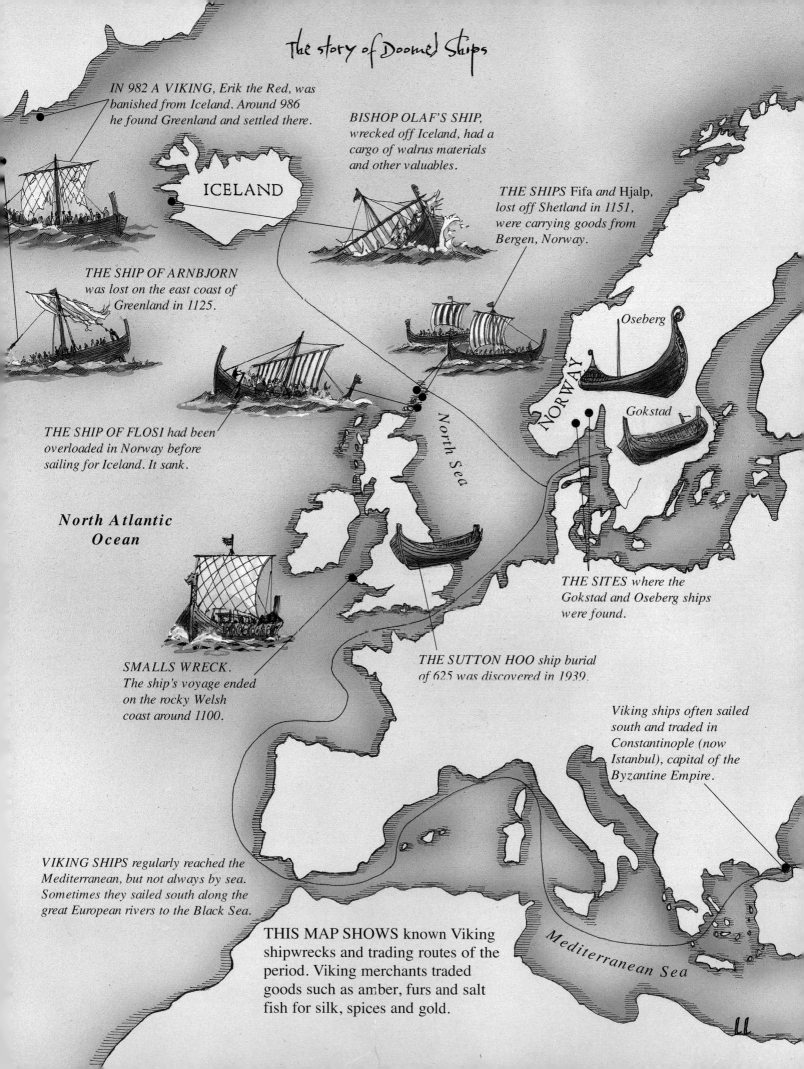

The story of Doomed Ships

IN 982 A VIKING, Erik the Red, was banished from Iceland. Around 986 he found Greenland and settled there.

BISHOP OLAF'S SHIP, wrecked off Iceland, had a cargo of walrus materials and other valuables.

ICELAND

THE SHIPS Fifa and Hjalp, lost off Shetland in 1151, were carrying goods from Bergen, Norway.

THE SHIP OF ARNBJORN was lost on the east coast of Greenland in 1125.

Oseberg

NORWAY

Gokstad

North Sea

THE SHIP OF FLOSI had been overloaded in Norway before sailing for Iceland. It sank.

North Atlantic Ocean

THE SITES where the Gokstad and Oseberg ships were found.

SMALLS WRECK. The ship's voyage ended on the rocky Welsh coast around 1100.

THE SUTTON HOO ship burial of 625 was discovered in 1939.

Viking ships often sailed south and traded in Constantinople (now Istanbul), capital of the Byzantine Empire.

VIKING SHIPS regularly reached the Mediterranean, but not always by sea. Sometimes they sailed south along the great European rivers to the Black Sea.

THIS MAP SHOWS known Viking shipwrecks and trading routes of the period. Viking merchants traded goods such as amber, furs and salt fish for silk, spices and gold.

Mediterranean Sea

BURIALS AND BURNINGS

Viking chief on his funeral pyre

NOT ALL DOOMED VIKING ships were wrecked – some became funeral pyres for dead chiefs. In 922 the Arab traveller Ibn Fadlan watched such a burning in Russia. The dead chief's favourite horses, dogs and slave were killed and put on board with him, then everything was set on fire.

Shipwreck on land!

Slave girl

Dead warrior

Tent

Mourners

In keeping with tradition, a naked man is the first to throw his torch

Sacrificed animals

Sacrifice of a slave

THE SLAVE CHOSEN to burn with her master had no choice; doomed, she must accept her fate.

THE CHIEF'S FAMILY and followers gathered around the ship. The fire was lit, then everyone tossed their lighted torches on board.

ARCHAEOLOGICAL evidence shows most ships used in mound burials were not seaworthy. Perhaps only old ships were used as funeral pyres.

Simple burials

ONLY IMPORTANT PEOPLE
had ship burials. Others might be
buried in a small boat or a grave
shaped like a boat. Most people
just had wood-lined pits.
Life was harsh and starving to
death in winter was a real
possibility. Men faced dangers at
sea, in battle, out hunting, or
when shipbuilding. Few lived
beyond the age of 45. If women
survived childbirth they might
reach 50.

*Only important Vikings were
buried or cremated in large ships.*

Furs

*Glass vase
and beaker*

*Persian
pottery*

Brazier

Spices

Goods for the grave

EVERYTHING the chief had
enjoyed when alive was put in
his grave for his new life: furs
for warmth, silk for fine clothes,
fragile glass vessels and metal
braziers, and spices for his food.

Angel of Death

THE 'ANGEL OF DEATH',
an old, black-clad woman, leaves
the funeral holding the knife she
used to kill the slave.

The 'Angel of Death'

13

FURTHER AND FURTHER

EUROPE

15th-century compass

COLUMBUS'S EPIC voyages across the Atlantic made people realise that long-distance expeditions were possible. Excited by the riches brought back from this 'New' World, European rulers funded more expeditions. As the most powerful countries in Europe in the 15th and 16th centuries, Spain and Portugal led the way. But, as the map shows, such voyages were very dangerous. There were no charts (sea maps) to warn of treacherous rocks and currents. Even when the lookout did spot them it was often too late to change course.

1673: THE PORTUGUESE carrack Jules was wrecked while returning to Lisbon from Goa loaded with pearls and amber.

South Atlantic Ocean

Watch out for reefs!

1559: RETURNING from India, the Framengo was wrecked on São Tomé, off west Africa.

I thought you were supposed to be on lookout!

But I can only see **above** the waves!

14

The story of Doomed Ships

ASIA

1609: To avoid capture, the Madre de Deus's *captain blows up his ship in Nagasaki Bay, Japan.*

IN THE 16TH AND 17TH centuries Canton was the great trading port of China.

1618: The Bacaim *sinks off the coast of India loaded with gold and spices.*

1511: The Flora de la Mar *sinks sailing to India with goods seized from Malacca.*

AFRICA

Indian Ocean

1561: STORMS off Sumatra wreck the **East Indiaman** *trading ship* São Paulo.

1601: A SHIP carrying silver coins sank near Kuantung when sailing between Goa and Macao.

1512: FRANCISCO SERRÃO'S trading ship loaded with coins sank between Malacca and the Spice Islands.

1590: BON JESUS, another East Indiaman, is wrecked on reefs sailing from Goa to Lisbon with a cargo of coins.

1589: LEAKING BADLY, the São Thomé *sailed from Cochin. It was soon wrecked. Hundreds died, but some people escaped in a longboat.*

1593: OVERLOADED with gold and silver, the Santo Alberto *sailed from Cochin, India. Wrecked close to shore, much of the cargo was salvaged.*

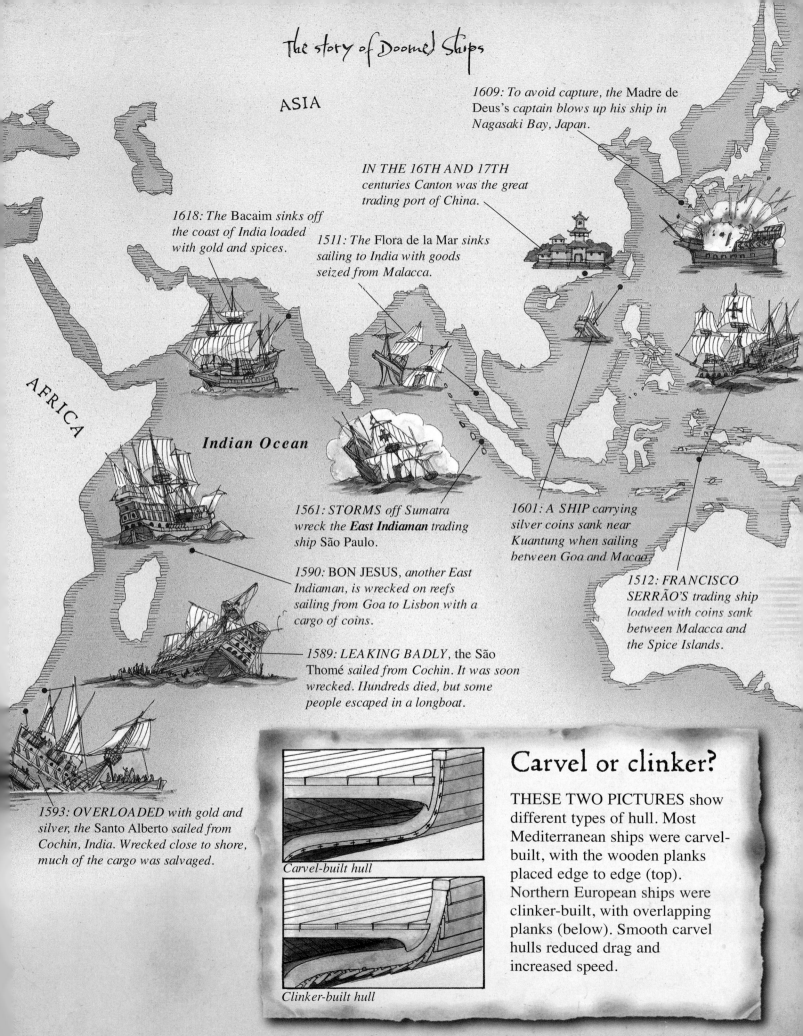

Carvel-built hull

Clinker-built hull

Carvel or clinker?

THESE TWO PICTURES show different types of hull. Most Mediterranean ships were carvel-built, with the wooden planks placed edge to edge (top). Northern European ships were clinker-built, with overlapping planks (below). Smooth carvel hulls reduced drag and increased speed.

PERILS OF EXPLORATION

16th-century
galleon

ARLY EXPLORERS faced problems long before setting sail. Columbus took years to raise the money for his voyage. Finding ships and crews could be difficult – usually only desperate men agreed to sail uncharted seas, perhaps never to return.

Stormy seas

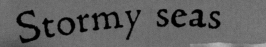

Small but mighty

15TH-CENTURY ships were tiny: Columbus's largest, the *Santa Maria*, was just 29 metres long. It shows the skill of captains and crews that so many ships survived all the dangers and returned to their home ports.

Magellan's misfortune

SEPTEMBER 1519: Disaster strikes Portuguese explorer Ferdinand Magellan's fleet as it sails west around the world. Storms sink one ship, and another, carrying most of the fleet's food, is forced to return to Spain.

Charting the uncharted

THIS MAP, drawn around 1480, shows just how little Europeans knew about the world. The Mediterranean is fairly accurate, and so is the west coast of Africa which Portuguese sailors had been exploring since 1418. Everything else is very vague. Sea maps are called charts, and early explorers really did sail in 'uncharted waters'.

In search of riches

WHY DID PEOPLE FUND and make these dangerous voyages? Money! Spices from Asia imported by land fetched high prices in Europe. If sea routes could be found to the east – the source of these spices – they would reach Europe more quickly and bring wealth to those who imported them. When Columbus reached land in 1492 he was convinced he'd reached Asia and the Indies, the source of spices and wealth. But he hadn't reached Asia at all – he had actually sailed to America.

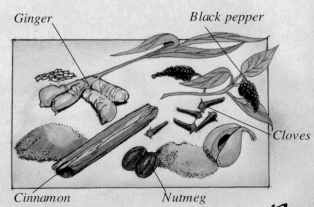

Ginger

Black pepper

Cloves

Cinnamon

Nutmeg

17

THE MARY ROSE

Sir George Carew, vice-admiral of Henry's fleet, went down with the Mary Rose

A MBITIOUS RULERS can be very dangerous for ships and their crews. One of the most ambitious was Henry VIII, king of England 1509–1547. Determined to outdo his rivals, especially the French King Louis XII, Henry ordered the building of two great warships, *Mary Rose* and *Great Harry*, in 1509. Henry's ships were each to have nearly 80 guns on board, to bombard enemy ships. Before that, warships had done little more than transport troops.

LAUNCHED IN 1511, the *Mary Rose* was the English fleet's **flagship**. Cutting holes in a ship's sides so that guns could fire through them was revolutionary. The early guns were not very accurate and sometimes blew up when fired. The gun ports gave the English a huge advantage – until the idea was copied, as it soon was.

Fortune of war

ON BOARD THE *MARY ROSE* were large quantities of gold angel coins (above). Each was worth more than a seaman earned in a whole month.

The world's greatest warships

I want guns! And lots of them!

Don't be too hasty, sire...

Bonaventure mizzen

Sterncastle deck

Sterncastle

Stern

Fighting top

Mizzenmast

Main topmast

Fore topmast

Mainmast

Foremast

Bowsprit

Anti-boarding nets

Spritsail

Forecastle

Forecastle deck

Weather deck

Bow

Gunports

Gun

Main gun deck

Orlop deck

Keel

Bigger and better?

BETWEEN 1536 AND 1540 *Mary Rose* and *Great Harry* were refitted (overhauled). Each was given a lower gun deck and room for more troops. The changes made them dangerously top-heavy.

19

LOST AND FOUND

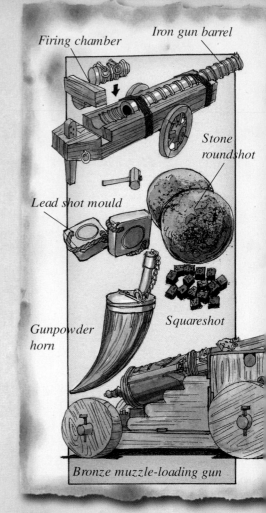

Firing chamber   Iron gun barrel

Stone roundshot

Lead shot mould

Squareshot

Gunpowder horn

Bronze muzzle-loading gun

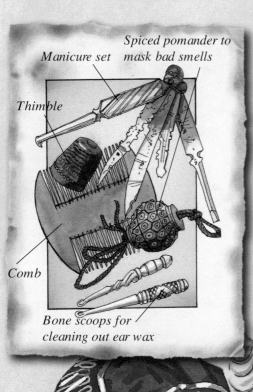

Tudor pocket sundial

Adding the lower gun deck to the *Mary Rose* was disastrous. On 19 July 1545 the ship suddenly heeled (tipped) to one side while sailing out of Portsmouth harbour to fight the French. Water poured through the open gunports and Henry VIII's flagship sank as he watched. Most of the 700 men on board drowned.

SILT AND WATER flooded into the *Mary Rose*, burying the ship and its contents. Time passed and the disaster was forgotten. Then, in 1968, divers discovered the wreck. Archaeological excavation uncovered hundreds of objects, from thimbles and combs (left) to guns (top right) and cooking pots.

Spiced pomander to mask bad smells

Manicure set

Thimble

Comb

Bone scoops for cleaning out ear wax

MY BEAUTIFUL SHIP!

Ooops!

The ship's surgeon

SILT COVERED the *Mary Rose* so quickly that everything on board was preserved in amazingly good condition. One exciting find was the equipment used by the ship's surgeon – including the mallet which he may have used to knock out patients before an operation! Anaesthetics would not be discovered for another four centuries. Like many ships' surgeons, the *Mary Rose*'s surgeon was also the ship's barber.

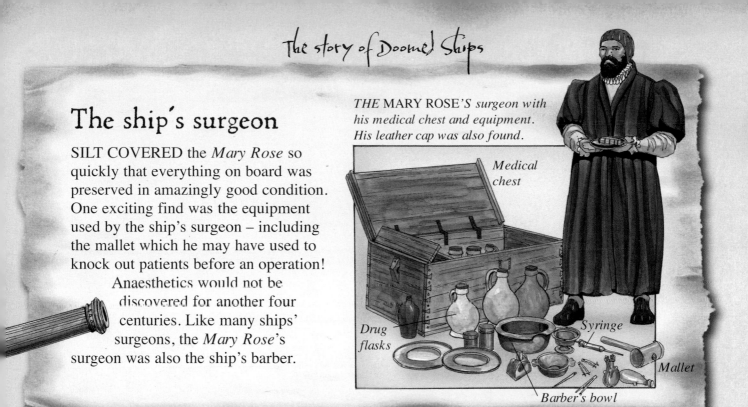

THE MARY ROSE'S *surgeon with his medical chest and equipment. His leather cap was also found.*

Medical chest

Drug flasks

Syringe

Mallet

Barber's bowl

There goes *Mary Rose!*

WHY DID THE *MARY ROSE* hccl over? A sudden gust of wind? Turning too sharply? No-one knows. We do know that the captain, Sir George Carew, went down with the ship.

Animals aboard

ALSO ON BOARD were large quantities of fleas, rats, lice and even a frog – archaeologists found their remains. The frog was meant to show the drinking water was fresh!

LOOK OUT: ARMADA!

PHILIP II OF SPAIN was angry with England. English seamen kept attacking his treasure ships returning from the Americas. Francis Drake had destroyed Spanish ships in Cádiz harbour. And England was no longer Roman Catholic, as it had been when Philip's wife, Mary I, was Queen. When she died in 1558 England became Protestant under Queen Elizabeth I. So Philip planned an attack by a great fleet, known as the **Spanish Armada**. But not all plans... go to plan.

Medal showing Elizabeth I

Not always plain sailing!

PURSUED BY STORMS and the English, many of the great Spanish ships were lost. Armed with 32 guns, La Juliana sank off the coast of Ireland.

LA TRINIDAD VALENCERA, *a converted grain ship, sank off Ireland's west coast.*

LA RATA ENCORONADA *also sank off western Ireland and was soon looted by local people.*

Philip II intended the Armada, his Spanish fleet, to sail up the English Channel, collect an army from the Low Countries and invade England. This map shows how his plan ended.

Maybe this wasn't such a good idea!

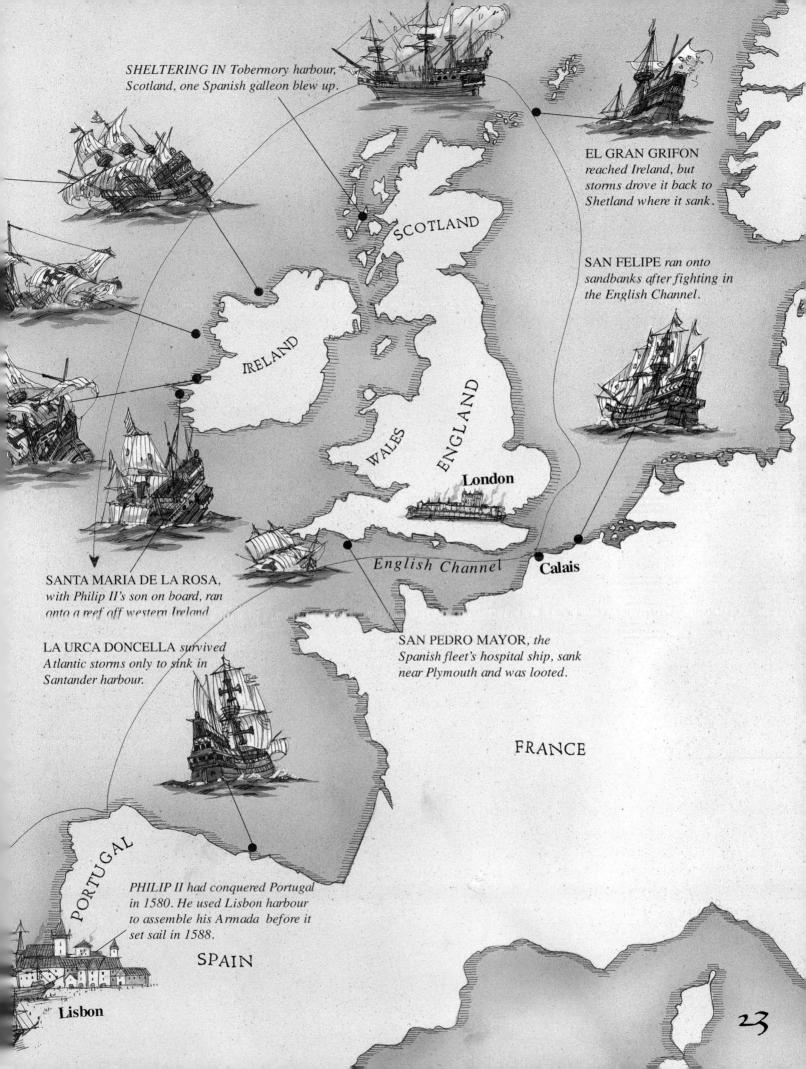

SHELTERING IN Tobermory harbour, Scotland, one Spanish galleon blew up.

EL GRAN GRIFON *reached Ireland, but storms drove it back to Shetland where it sank.*

SAN FELIPE *ran onto sandbanks after fighting in the English Channel.*

SCOTLAND

IRELAND

WALES

ENGLAND

London

English Channel

Calais

FRANCE

SANTA MARIA DE LA ROSA, *with Philip II's son on board, ran onto a reef off western Ireland*

LA URCA DONCELLA *survived Atlantic storms only to sink in Santander harbour.*

SAN PEDRO MAYOR, *the Spanish fleet's hospital ship, sank near Plymouth and was looted.*

PORTUGAL

PHILIP II *had conquered Portugal in 1580. He used Lisbon harbour to assemble his* Armada *before it set sail in 1588.*

SPAIN

Lisbon

23

ENGLISH TACTICS

Spanish officers

THE ENGLISH HAD smaller ships than the Spanish, but they were more manoeuvrable. The Spanish fleet sailed up the English Channel in crescent formation. They were too strong for an English attack, so the English just harassed them. On 27 July 1588 the Spanish anchored at Calais in France. The English remained nearby. The next night the English sent **fire ships** among the tightly packed Spanish ships. Panic-stricken, the Spanish cut their moorings and scattered in utter confusion.

The English admiral Sir Francis Drake – El Draco (the Dragon) to the Spanish

THE SPANISH had six galleasses: part sailing ship, part galley. Useful in the calm Mediterranean, they were useless in Atlantic storms. Officers and overseers (above) supervised the oarsmen. These men didn't fight, but took up space that could have been used for extra guns. The English had no galleasses: only sailing warships.

English fire ships

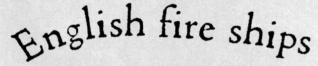

SAILING FIRE SHIPS was dangerous: you had to sail among the enemy's ships, light a slow fuse and escape – fast.

What's that smell? The cook must be burning dinner again!

Royal arms of
England

The galleon Ark Royal

Bow

Poop
(stern) deck

Gunports and
cannon

Rudder

Loading a cannon

Skilful sailors

WELL-TRAINED crews made all
the difference in battle. Seamen
called master gunners organised
ships' guns and gun crews. The
faster the sailors fired and
reloaded the gun, the better the
chance of damaging the enemy's
ships. Naval battles were noisy
and confusing, and smoke from
the guns made it hard to see.

Lighter and lower: Galleons

AFTER THE *MARY ROSE* disaster, English warships became
lighter and, most importantly, lower, so they were less likely to
heel over in strong winds. Known as galleons, these ships were the
most important trading and fighting ships of the 16th century. The
Ark Royal (above), the English flagship used against the Armada,
was a galleon.

Picture showing the English attacking the Spanish Armada, 1588

25

UTTER DISASTER!

A**TTACKED BY THE** English fire ships, the Spanish Armada was in disarray. It could not sail back down the English Channel because the English were blocking it. Then storms blew up. Facing gales, high seas and attacks by the English, the Spanish ships sailed north and around the British Isles. Many were wrecked as they did so.

Spanish soldiers from the Armada ships

Shipwrecked

THE SPANISH were good sailors – by 1588 they had been sailing the Atlantic successfully for nearly 100 years. But they had little experience of the northern coasts of Britain, and hundreds of Spanish sailors died in shipwrecks.

All washed up

Take my hand, these English waters are cold!

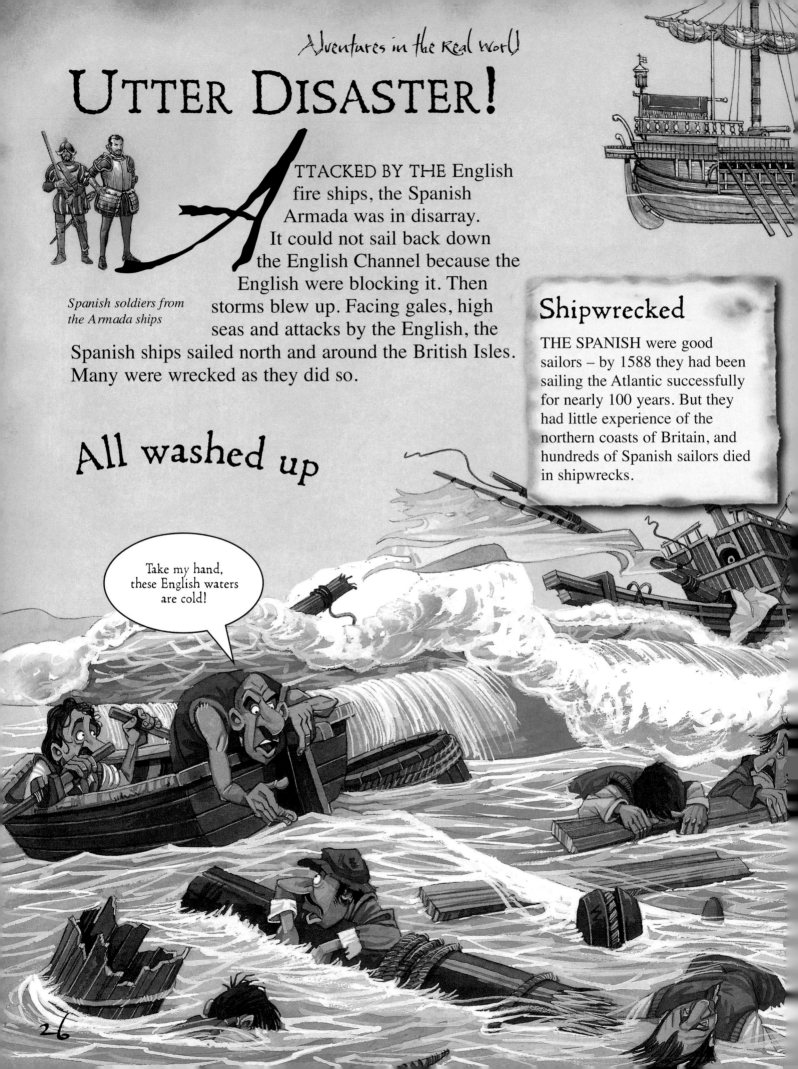

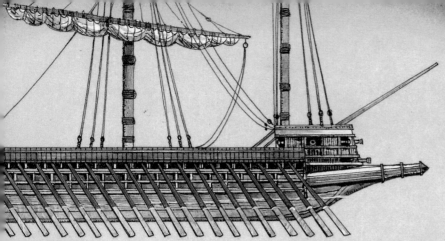

THE SIX GALLEASSES in the Spanish fleet were hybrids – part rowed galleys and part sailing galleons. After the Armada disaster they were rarely used again.

Poor leadership?

PHILIP CHOSE the Duke of Medina Sidonia to lead the Armada. It was a bad choice. Storms and English seamen like Sir Francis Drake were too much for him. But he did manage to get the flagship *San Martín*, and half the Armada, back to Lisbon in Portugal.

The San Martín

Spanish survivors

IN A CRASH of splintering wood and tearing sails, the Spanish galleass, *La Girona*, was wrecked on the rocks at Dunluce on the northern Irish coast. Wrecks provided plunder for coastal towns and villages.

Many of the Spanish sailors who survived the Armada shipwrecks never got home to Spain, and probably settled in Britain. Were they the dark, handsome strangers of so many legends?

27

PIRATE WRECKS

The skull and crossed swords of a pirate's flag

IT WAS DANGEROUS being a **pirate**. You faced the dangers of the sea and, because you owed allegiance to no-one, you were everyone's enemy. So why did men (and it was mostly men) become pirates?

Money, greed, excitement, independence – some or all of these played a part. **Privateers** were slightly different. They acted like pirates – seizing ships that belonged to other people – but they did it with the permission of a ruler (who pretended to know nothing about it).

Villains... or heroes?

WHETHER SOMEONE was a pirate or a privateer depended which side you were on. To the Spanish, Francis Drake was a pirate because he kept capturing their treasure ships. But he was encouraged by Elizabeth I, so to the English he was a privateer – and a hero.

IN 1589 a Spanish ship captured by the Earl of Cumberland was wrecked on the Cornish cliffs.

EUROPE

THE WHYDAH, pirate Sam Bellamy's ship, sank off Cape Cod in 1717, taking with it a cargo of gold and silver.

THE OXFORD, pirate Henry Morgan's flagship, blew up in the West Indies in 1669.

ONE OF THE RICHEST treasure ships from the East, Las Chagas, was sunk by English pirates in 1594.

SUNK BY English pirates near the Azores, Nuestra Señora de Guía carried gold, silver and pearls.

HENRY MORGAN sank the Magdalena in 1669. He salvaged 15,000 of the 40,000 coins it was carrying.

ENGLISH PIRATES captured the Rosario as it sailed to Panama in 1681. They thought its cargo was tin, and left it on board. But the 'tin' was really silver!

Yargh! Where be the gold ship?

South Atlantic Ocean

SOUTH AMERICA

Mary Read

Blackbeard

Ann Bonny

Henry Morgan

EDWARD TEACH or Thatch, nicknamed Blackbeard, was the terror of shipping in the West Indies and along America's east coast. In 1718 his ship was captured. He was beheaded and most of his crew hanged.

MARY READ, who dressed as a man, joined the army. It was too dull so she joined the ship of 'Calico Jack' Rackham. Ann Bonny, Jack's wife, also dressed like a man. Caught in 1720, Jack was hanged and the women imprisoned.

PIRATE HENRY MORGAN attacked Spain's ships in the West Indies. But England and Spain were at peace, so Charles II of England arrested him. When the peace ended, Charles gave Morgan an official post in the West Indies!

THE BARBARY PIRATES, led by the Barbarossa brothers, terrorised ships along the North African coast in the 16th century.

ASIA

IN 1800 French privateer Robert Surcouf boarded the Kent, *an English East Indiaman, off India. He threw the cargo of gold overboard.*

AFRICA

Arabian Sea

THE SAMARITAN, *one of a privateering fleet sailing to the Indian Ocean in 1635, sank near the Comoros Islands.*

IN 1689 FRENCH privateers blew up the East Indiaman Herbert *and its cargo of silver.*

South China Sea

THE SPEAKER, *pirate John Bowen's ship, sank off Mauritius in 1702. Survivors paid the island's governor 2,100 **pieces of eight** to go free.*

IN 1407 THE CHINESE explorer Cheng Ho sank the ship of Ch'en Tsu-i when he attacked a fleet off the Sumatran coast.

29

DANGER – PIRATES!

17th-century pistol

THERE HAVE BEEN pirates ever since merchant ships with valuable cargos set sail. In the eastern Mediterranean archaeologists have excavated 3,000-year-old ships sunk by pirates. Piracy was worst in the 17th and 18th centuries, especially in the Caribbean Sea where the treasure ships sailing from the Americas to Europe provided rich prizes. Even today pirates are a problem, especially in the Far East where they use high-powered speedboats and powerful guns to attack oil tankers and other ships, sometimes holding ship and crew to **ransom**.

Hide and seek

SLOOPS (ABOVE) WERE popular with pirates. They were small ships (10 to 20 metres), had up to 12 guns and could carry 150 men. But their biggest advantage was that their hulls were shallow, so they could hide in small bays and inlets where large ships could not reach them.

Pirates off the port bow!

ROYAL WRECK

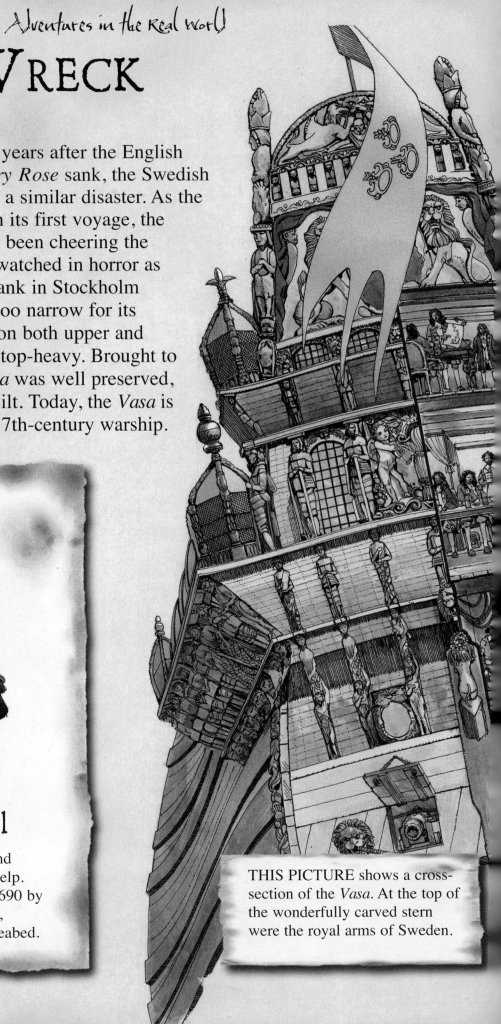

Carving from the Vasa

IN 1628, 83 years after the English flagship *Mary Rose* sank, the Swedish navy suffered a similar disaster. As the *Vasa* set sail on its first voyage, the crowds who had been cheering the magnificent ship watched in horror as it heeled over and sank in Stockholm harbour. The ship was too narrow for its length and had heavy guns on both upper and lower gun decks, making it top-heavy. Brought to the surface in 1961, the *Vasa* was well preserved, protected by the harbour's silt. Today, the *Vasa* is the world's only complete 17th-century warship.

Halley's Diving Bell

HUMANS NEED air to survive and cannot work underwater without help. Halley's diving bell, invented in 1690 by Edmund Halley, trapped air inside, allowing humans to work on the seabed.

THIS PICTURE shows a cross-section of the *Vasa*. At the top of the wonderfully carved stern were the royal arms of Sweden.

New technology, new discoveries

HALLEY'S DIVING BELL was a first step towards modern diving technology. In 1819, Augustus Siebe invented the diving suit (right) with air pumped into the helmet under pressure to keep seawater out. As technology improved, divers could work at greater depths.

The continuing development of modern equipment means that wrecks like the *Vasa* and the *Mary Rose* can be excavated underwater before being raised. Once at the surface, the ships are kept in special conditions and sprayed to stop the timbers from crumbling.

Augustus Siebe's diving suit

THE WARSHIP *VASA* was built for Gustavus Adolphus, king of Sweden (1611–1632). The ship carried 64 guns on two decks. There was an attempt to raise the *Vasa* when it first sank, but it failed and the ship was abandoned.

REDISCOVERED IN 1956, the *Vasa* was buried in about 33 metres of mud. About 16,000 items, and the skeletons of some of the sailors, were salvaged from it.

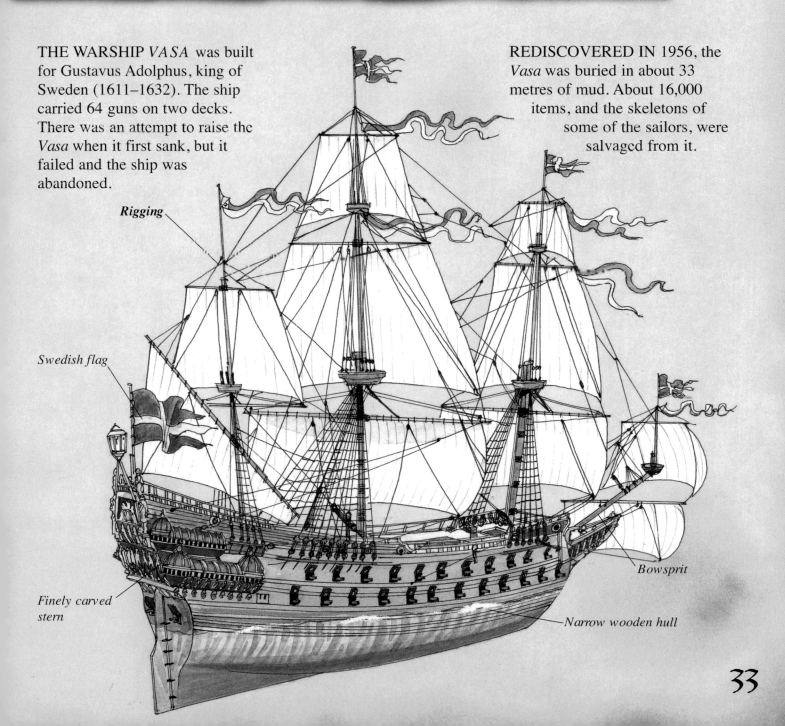

Rigging

Swedish flag

Finely carved stern

Bowsprit

Narrow wooden hull

WRECKS AND RICHES

The arms of the British East India Company

IN THE 16TH CENTURY, Spain dominated the sea and trade with the Americas. But by the 17th century the Dutch and English were the European sea powers and they traded with the Far East. The English founded an East India Company in 1600; the Dutch followed in 1602. These hugely profitable companies used big trading ships, known as East Indiamen. The ships carried metals such as gold, silver and copper as well as woollen textiles, watches and guns from Europe to India. They returned to Europe with spices, silk, carpets, gems and tea.

Stuck fast!

1737: The Vendela, *a Danish East Indiaman with a cargo of silver, was wrecked off the Shetland Islands.*

1749: THE AMSTERDAM *ran aground near Hastings, England.*

IN 1798 THE HARTWELL *was wrecked on its way to the Cape Verde Islands to punish mutineers.*

THE BRITANNIA, *sailing from Brazil in 1805, struck reefs and sank. One sailor survived.*

GUNPOWDER WAS a dangerous cargo. In 1800 the Queen *blew up near Bahia, Brazil.*

South Atlantic Ocean

1613: PORTUGUESE ships blow up Witte Leeuw *as it returns to Europe with diamonds and rare Chinese porcelain.*

She's not going to budge!

On its **maiden voyage** in 1749, the Dutch East India Company ship *Amsterdam* ran aground off the coast of Hastings, England.

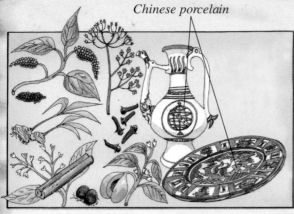

Chinese porcelain

Herbs and spices

Oriental tastes

Here are some of the spices that had first prompted long-distance voyages by Europeans, and then became the basis of the East India trade. Chinese porcelain also became very popular and was a luxury that fetched high prices in Europe.

ASIA

AFRICA

Arabian Sea

South China Sea

Indian Ocean

AUSTRALIA

THE FREDRICK ADOLPHUS, *with 39 boxes of silver, sank in the South China Sea in 1791.*

1772: SUNK by a typhoon off China, the Rysburgh's *cargo of silver was saved, but sharks ate eight sailors.*

1725: WRECKED off the Maldives, nine cargo chests were saved from the Ravenstein.

WITH THE MONSOON *behind it, the* Winterton *hit reefs off Madagascar in 1792.*

THE GELDERMALSEN *sank in 1752. Its cargo of porcelain was salvaged 200 years later.*

1744: The Saint Gérain *was lost off Mauritius.*

1681: LUXURIES for Louis XIV of France go down with the Soleil d'Orient *off Madagascar.*

1629: THE BATAVIA was lost when a storm smashed it against rocks off Australia's west coast.

1782: THE GROSVENOR sinks off Africa, taking with it East India Company jewels.

35

EAST INDIAMEN AHOY!

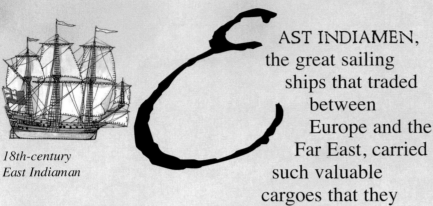

*18th-century
East Indiaman*

AST INDIAMEN, the great sailing ships that traded between Europe and the Far East, carried such valuable cargoes that they were often as well armed as warships. In 1804 Nathaniel Dance, a British commodore, was leading a convoy of 16 East Indiamen and 12 smaller ships when French government warships threatened them. Dance saw them off, got the convoy safely home and became a national hero.

It pays to trade!

EAST INDIAMEN were more than just merchant ships – they were prestige vessels. And so the living quarters, at least for officers, were much more comfortable than in most other ships. Even the crews were better fed on East Indiamen. The rewards for completing a successful voyage were immense for everyone involved – which was another reason why everyone on board wanted to see off pirates and other attackers!

Cutaway view of an 18th-century East Indiaman

Crew's quarters

The deep hull allowed plenty of room for storing goods.

Cargo hold

Model of a tea porter

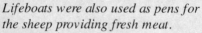

239

PORTERS CARRYING TEA to ships in eastern ports were a familiar sight to European crewmen. Tea was particularly valuable in the 18th century, when it became a fashionable drink in Europe. This model recalls that trade.

*17TH-CENTURY chart of the route into New Holland, a Dutch **colony** in America. The place still exists – it's now New York.*

Grand designs

SHIPS SAIL perfectly well without ornamental sterns. But this carving on the *Prins Willem*, a Dutch East India Company ship, reflected national pride.

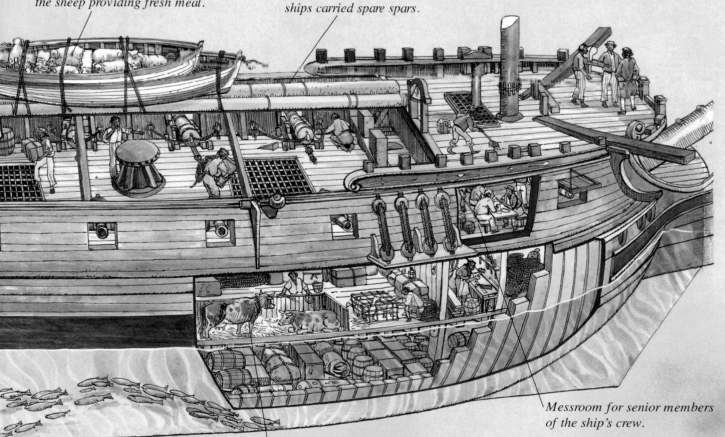

Lifeboats were also used as pens for the sheep providing fresh meat.

A ship with damaged masts or spars was hard to sail and easy for enemies to board. So all ships carried spare spars.

Messroom for senior members of the ship's crew.

Cows kept below deck provided fresh milk.

WRECKS OF REVOLUTION

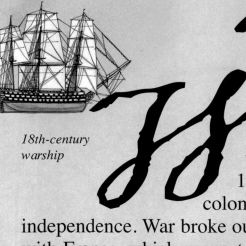

18th-century warship

WAR AND REVOLUTION dominated Europe and North America at the end of the 18th century. In 1776, Britain's American colonies declared independence. War broke out with the colonies and with France, which supported the colonists. Britain lost and in 1783 the United States of America was founded. A few years later in 1789, France faced its own revolution and another war with Britain. Navies were crucially important to protect merchant shipping. Although efficient convoy systems were developed, many ships were wrecked.

North Atlantic Ocean

NORTH AMERICA

IN 1763 the Hussar, a 28-gun **frigate**, was becalmed off New York. Later it drifted, hit a rock and sank.

Bushnell's *Turtle*

DESIGNED BY American David Bushnell in 1776, the *Turtle* became the first **submersible** to attack a surface warship. During the American revolutionary wars, the *Turtle* tried to fix explosives to British HMS *Eagle*'s hull. The attack failed because the hulls of the British ships were covered in copper.

THE HMS DE BRAAR, *a sloop with 14 guns, sank off Delaware in 1798. Almost everyone on board drowned.*

SUBMARINES soon improved. In February 1864, during the American Civil War, the CSS *Hunley* sank the USS *Housatonic*. Unfortunately the *Hunley* also sank.

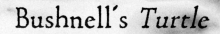

Submarine Hunley, *1864*

Breathing valve

Torpedo (underwater bomb)

Sailors turning propeller

IN 1779 BONHOMME RICHARD, a Franco-American ship, sank off the coast of northern Britain after a fight with the British.

1790: THE TELEMAQUE sinks along with the valuables of aristocrats fleeing the French Revolution.

THE ZEELILIE, a Dutch East Indiaman sailing from Ireland to England, was wrecked off the Isles of Scilly.

1806: POLLUCE, a Spanish treasure ship fleeing Napoleon's French navy, sinks off the Island of Elba.

THE GALLEON Mercedes was blown up by the British. The wreck, and its cargo of gold and silver, have never been found.

SAILING FROM GIBRALTAR to Malta in 1806, the British warship Athénienne hit rocks off Sicily and sank.

1798: THE FRENCH flagship L'Orient was blown up by the British fleet under Admiral Nelson in Aboukir Bay, Egypt, during the battle of the Nile.

GREAT BRITAIN

FRANCE

SPAIN

Mediterranean Sea

Black Sea

Front-loading cannons

EIGHTEENTH-CENTURY naval guns were front-loading: gunpowder was rammed down the barrel and held in place with a felt wad. The ammunition followed, and then more wadding. When this was done, the fuse was lit and the gun fired.

Match

Ramrod

Front-loading cannon

Ropes to control recoil

MYTH OR REALITY?

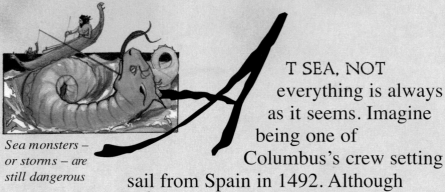

Sea monsters – or storms – are still dangerous

AT SEA, NOT everything is always as it seems. Imagine being one of Columbus's crew setting sail from Spain in 1492. Although Columbus hadn't told you his exact plans, you knew you were in for a long voyage. In fact you would be sailing into waters where neither your captain nor the crew had been before. What would you find? Would you ever get home? Always looking out for danger, narrowing your eyes against the glare of sun on sea – and probably short of food and sleep – is it any wonder you saw amazing sights? But were they real?

Mer-myths

LONG BEFORE Columbus set sail, the ancient Greeks explored the Mediterranean in their galleys. The myth of Odysseus (Ulysses to the Romans) reflects these voyages. He took ten years to sail home after the Trojan War. Was he just a bad sailor or did he face real problems? The myth says that Sirens (below) lived on the coast near Sicily, luring men to their deaths with their song. It seems much more likely that the rocky coast itself killed the men.

The voyage of Odysseus

A catchy tune, but it's a one-hit wonder!

Real monsters?

MANY SEA MONSTERS reported by early sailors were imaginary, but not all. Blue whales, which weigh about 120 tonnes, seen from ships like Columbus's *Santa Maria* (weight 100 tonnes), would have seemed truly monstrous.

Stranger than fiction!

SOME SEA MONSTERS exist in fact as well as myth. The giant squid is one, but is seldom caught alive. Would anyone believe you if you said you'd seen a creature with cone-shaped body 6 metres long and even longer tentacles?

Giant squid

Over six metres long!

The mythical Kraken

Tales of the Kraken

THE MYTH of the Kraken is probably based on a confusion between the octopus and the rare giant squid of the ocean depths. In the myth, the giant Kraken (left) wraps sailing ships in its terrifyingly long, strong tentacles and drags ship and crew to their doom in the depths of the ocean. As long-distance voyages increased, so did sailors' knowledge of real sea creatures, and so tales of terrifying monsters became fewer.

GHOST SHIPS

The Mary Celeste

THE DISTANCE ACROSS the Atlantic or Pacific Oceans is the same for modern container ships as it was for 15th-century Portuguese carracks. The earlier ships just took longer to cover the same distance and, crucially, had no way of summoning help if things went wrong. And go wrong they did, so it's no surprise there are tales of ghost ships. Sometimes a 'ghost ship' was actually just a real ship that had been blown off course and was spotted in an unexpected location... but not always.

A cold case?

NOT ALL MYSTERIES involve ghost ships. It is said that in 1761 the *Octavius* sailed from England to the North-West Passage, probably headed for China. Without today's navigation or communication systems, something clearly went wrong, because it was lost for 13 years. It was supposedly rediscovered in 1775. Everything at first seemed normal – except that the crew were frozen solid.

Frozen for 13 years!

They're giving us the cold shoulder...

What an icy reception!

The mythical Flying Dutchman

Flight of fancy

THE *FLYING DUTCHMAN* is perhaps the best-known myth of the sea. Like most myths, it has several versions. The basic story tells of a Dutch sea captain who is cursed to sail the oceans until he finds a woman whose love will set him free. Every seven years he can land to search for her. The one thing that doesn't change in the various versions is the nationality of the sea captain, showing what great sailors and traders the Dutch were.

The Mary Celeste

The Mary Celeste

THE *MARY CELESTE* was a real ship, with real people on it. On 5 November 1872, Captain Benjamin Briggs left New York with his wife, their baby daughter and a crew of seven. On 25 November they sailed south of the Azores, as he recorded. Early in December another ship noticed something odd about *Mary Celeste* and sent a boarding party. There was no-one on board, no sign of a fight or a fire, and the ship's boats had gone. What had happened? That remains a mystery.

43

WHALING SHIP ESSEX

The fluke (tail) of Melville's Moby Dick

WHALING BEGAN IN EUROPEAN seas in the 10th century. Since then it has spread around the world. What began as a fairly even contest between large whales and small boats armed with hand-held harpoons has become entirely one-sided – nowadays, huge whaling ships armed with explosive harpoons hunt rapidly declining numbers of whales. Very occasionally a whale hits back: a huge sperm whale attacked and sank the whaling ship *Essex* in 1820. Tales like this inspired Herman Melville's *Moby Dick*, which tells of Captain Ahab's hunt for revenge after he loses a leg to a great white whale.

When whales fight back!

ABOUT A WEEK after the *Essex* sank, some of the surviving crew had to endure another whale attack. A killer whale attacked one of the small whaleboats in which the crew had escaped, but luckily the boat did not sink.

They don't call them 'killer' whales for nothing!

44

The plight of the *Essex*

THE WHALING SHIP *ESSEX* was sunk by a sperm whale on 20 November 1820. Although the crew survived by boarding the *Essex*'s three small whaleboats, they had salvaged only a few provisions. After spending many months stranded in the Pacific Ocean with practically no food or water, the crew began to resort to desperate measures to stay alive: cannibalism! Two of the boats were eventually rescued in February 1821 – only eight of the twenty crewmen survived.

The Essex is rammed by a whale.

One whaleboat is attacked by a killer whale.

Crew find Henderson Island but don't stay.

One boat is rescued by the Indian.

The boats are separated in a storm and one boat disappears.

Remaining boat rescued 23 Feb 1821

PACIFIC OCEAN

Cape Horn

Map showing the journey of the Essex *around the coast of South America in 1820*

THE BRITISH BEGAN whaling in the southern Pacific Ocean in 1787, and the Americans quickly followed. The cold currents flowing north from the Antarctic held huge quantities of krill, which attracted large numbers of whales.

A sperm whale attacks the Essex, *1820*

FULL STEAM AHEAD!

THE DOMINANCE of the East Indiamen was challenged in the late 19th century. Wind, on which sailing ships depended, is an unreliable power source. Steam engines, invented at the end of the 18th century, could provide power that was reliable and efficient – although at first it was neither, so early steamships had sails too. But in 1838, the *Sirius* made the first steam-powered Atlantic crossing. Improved engines and hulls made of iron instead of wood followed fast – the era of modern shipping had begun.

The Friedrich Wilhelm, *an early steam-powered passenger boat*

THE LINER Prins Frederik *sank off the Bay of Biscay in 1890.*

THE TITANIC *(see pages 48–51)*

THE ANDREA DORIA *hit the* Stockholm *and sank off New York in 1956.*

1852: THE AMAZON'S *engines overheated in the Bay of Biscay on its maiden voyage.*

SOUTH AMERICA

1892: THE STEAMSHIP John Elder *and its cargo of gold and silver were lost off Chile.*

South Atlantic Ocean

How fast are we going?

Around 22.5 **knots!**

MAGNIFICENT LINERS carried passengers across the Atlantic early in the 20th century. One of the finest was the American White Star Line's *Titanic*. The *Titanic* was hailed as 'unsinkable', even before its first voyage.

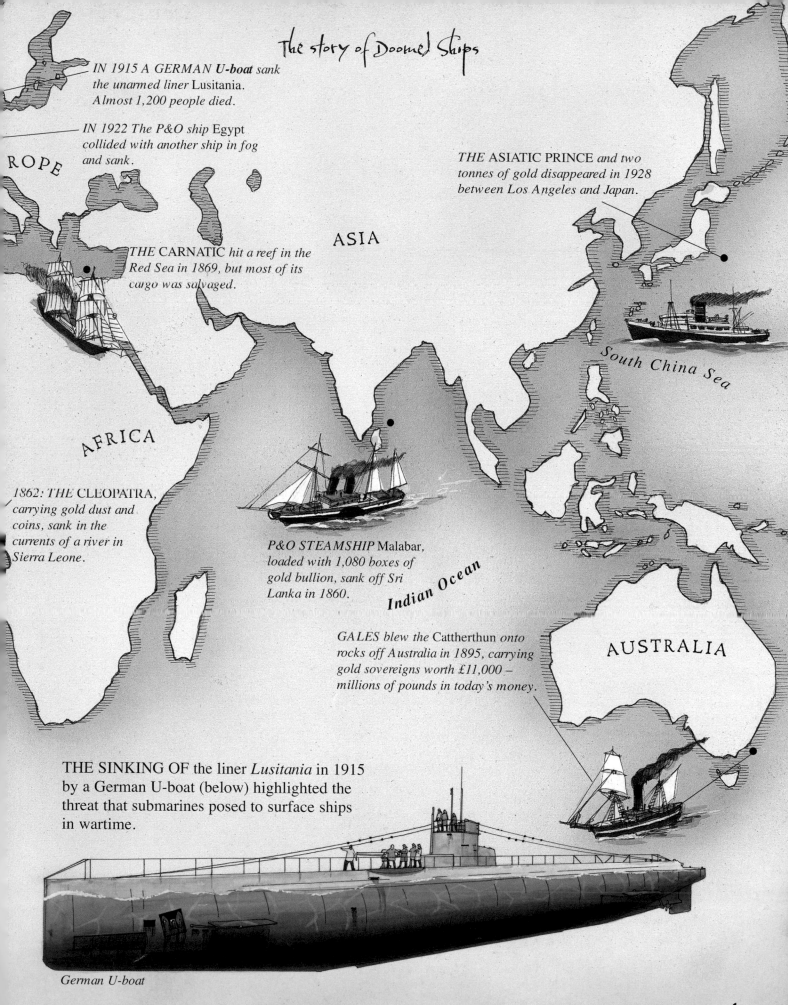

The story of Doomed Ships

IN 1915 A GERMAN **U-boat** sank the unarmed liner Lusitania. Almost 1,200 people died.

IN 1922 The P&O ship Egypt collided with another ship in fog and sank.

THE ASIATIC PRINCE and two tonnes of gold disappeared in 1928 between Los Angeles and Japan.

ROPE

ASIA

THE CARNATIC hit a reef in the Red Sea in 1869, but most of its cargo was salvaged.

South China Sea

AFRICA

1862: THE CLEOPATRA, carrying gold dust and coins, sank in the currents of a river in Sierra Leone.

P&O STEAMSHIP Malabar, loaded with 1,080 boxes of gold bullion, sank off Sri Lanka in 1860.

Indian Ocean

GALES blew the Cattherthun onto rocks off Australia in 1895, carrying gold sovereigns worth £11,000 – millions of pounds in today's money.

AUSTRALIA

THE SINKING OF the liner *Lusitania* in 1915 by a German U-boat (below) highlighted the threat that submarines posed to surface ships in wartime.

German U-boat

DANGER – ICEBERG!

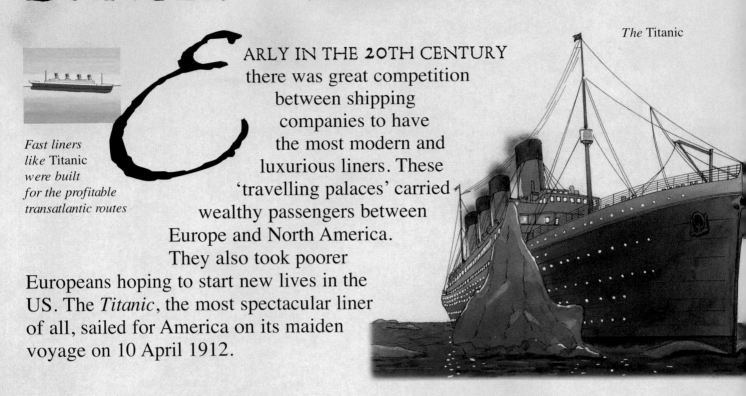

The Titanic

EARLY IN THE **20**TH CENTURY there was great competition between shipping companies to have the most modern and luxurious liners. These 'travelling palaces' carried wealthy passengers between Europe and North America. They also took poorer Europeans hoping to start new lives in the US. The *Titanic*, the most spectacular liner of all, sailed for America on its maiden voyage on 10 April 1912.

Fast liners like Titanic *were built for the profitable transatlantic routes*

The first – and final – voyage

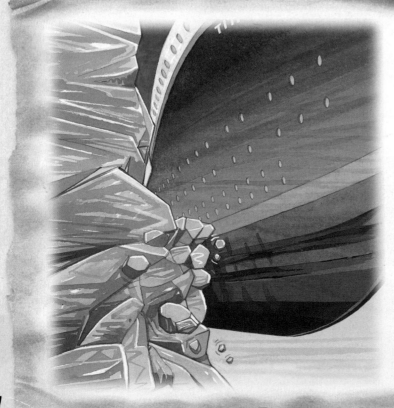

An unseen threat

THE *TITANIC* had been built to such high safety standards that no-one thought it could sink. But, at 11.40pm on 14 April, a lookout saw an iceberg ahead. The ship turned and missed it, but the 'berg had an underwater spur. This tore a gash over 90 metres long in *Titanic*'s side, puncturing six of the watertight compartments designed to keep the ship afloat. No ship could survive such damage.

As they melt, icebergs may flip over and show darker patches of ice, making them hard to see at night. The enquiry into *Titanic*'s loss suggested this had happened.

THE DINING SALOON for first-class passengers could seat 500 people. But the lower you went in the ship, the cheaper and more cramped the accommodation became.

SOME SAID *Titanic* was trying to break the speed record across the Atlantic. This was untrue – the ship did not carry enough fuel to do so.

SADLY, IF THE *TITANIC* had hit the iceberg head-on instead of turning to avoid it, it would probably have suffered less damage and not sunk.

49

'GREAT LOSS OF LIFE'

Flag of the White Star line

SO READ THE HEADLINE of a London newspaper reporting the *Titanic*'s sinking. It was not exaggerating: of 2,201 people on board, only 712 were rescued from the lifeboats by the liner *Carpathia*, the first ship on the scene. The rest died in *Titanic* or in the Atlantic's icy waters.

More people might have survived if there had been more lifeboats on board. There were just enough to meet regulations and to provide places for 1,178 people, but few of the lifeboats were full. Since *Titanic*'s loss, ships have been required by law to have lifeboats for everyone on board.

Titanic goes under

So much for being 'unsinkable'!

TITANIC

United States

THE *BLUE RIBBON* (or *Riband*) was awarded annually for the fastest transatlantic sea crossing. The record, 35.59 knots, was set in 1952 by the *United States*. Now aircraft fly the Atlantic at speeds impossible for ships.

Titanic's last hours

11.45pm

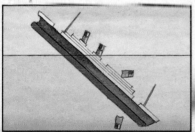

11.50pm

11.45pm: Water floods into the bow through the gash in the **starboard** side, making the ship front-heavy.

11.50pm: The weight at the bow lifts the stern out of the water.

Around midnight: The weight of the stern raised in the air breaks *Titanic* in two.

Moments later: As the bow sinks the stern crashes down, then rears up as water floods in.

2.20am: Last sight of *Titanic* as its stern sinks.

4.00am: The *Carpathia* reaches the scene and rescues survivors.

Needless delays

BECAUSE NO-ONE thought *Titanic* would sink, the crew was slow to launch the lifeboats and the passengers were even slower to get into them. Many boats were launched before they were full. Fortunately for those in them, the sea was calm.

Lost in the depths?

THE ATLANTIC is 4,000 metres deep where *Titanic* sank. Would the wreck ever be found? It was – on 1 September 1985. A team of French and American scientists with submersibles studied the wreck, photographing and filming it from every angle. But the one part they wanted to see was invisible. *Titanic*'s bow lies on its starboard side, hiding the damage done by the iceberg. At that depth, it will probably remain another of the sea's secrets.

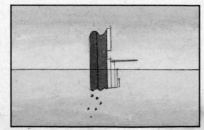

Midnight

2.00 am

RACING TO THE POLES

The North Pole

BY THE END OF the 19th century geographers had charted the edges of the Arctic in the north and the Antarctic in the south. But no-one had reached either North or South Pole. The cost of such expeditions was so high that only governments could afford to fund them – and so they did. In fact it became a matter of intense national pride as to which country's expedition would reach the poles first.

Sailing through ice? Whatever next!

A frozen ocean

THE DANGERS OF POLAR exploration were enormous. The bad weather was unpredictable, but the ice was probably more dangerous, especially with wooden ships. In summer, the edges of the polar ice sheets melt a little and break up, so ships can get closer to the Poles. But the melted passages do not remain ice-free for long. If ships became trapped in the ice they might be crushed by its power – that could mean a slow, lonely death.

Engine

Boilers

Scott's cabin

Fuel store

Crew's
quarters

Galley

Bows strengthened
to withstand ice

DISCOVERY

Robert Falcon Scott

Robert Scott

IN 1901 CAPTAIN Robert
Falcon Scott led the first British
expedition to Antarctica.
He returned safely in 1904 with
much information about the
continent. On his second
expedition (1910–1912) he
reached the South Pole, but
discovered that Norwegian
explorer Roald Amundsen had
got there a month earlier. Caught
in appalling weather (even by
Antarctic standards), he and his
team could not get back to the
Discovery (top), the ship he used
for his polar expeditions, and
died slowly of cold and
exhaustion.

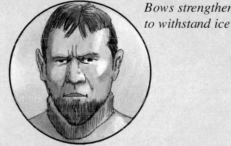

Ernest Shackleton

Ernest Shackleton

ERNEST SHACKLETON took
part in Scott's first Antarctic
expedition. In 1909 he led his
own team there, almost reaching
the South Pole before conditions
forced him back. In 1915, when
his ship *Endurance* became
trapped in the ice, he and five
others set out to get help – a
journey of 1,300 kilometres in
some of the most hostile
conditions humans have ever
survived. He died in 1922 on his
fourth Antarctic expedition.

A new challenge

THE ANTARCTIC is a
landmass, unlike the Arctic
which is an immense sheet of
ice floating on the sea.
Reaching the South Pole was
an even greater challenge than
getting to the North Pole,
because Antarctica is so far
from the European countries
involved in polar exploration.

The South Pole

53

SEA WOLVES THREATEN

U-boat commander's cap

EVER SINCE 1864, when the *Hunley* sank an enemy ship, surface ships have feared the underwater menace. Submarines, used in both World Wars, were a particular threat to an island like the United Kingdom which imported much of its food. The German submarine (U-boat) fleets were nicknamed 'sea wolves' because, like wolves, they hunted in packs. But the **Allies** had submarines too, so the underwater battle began.

Designed to sink!

DURING World War Two, merchant ships would often travel in groups, or convoys, to lessen the risk of being attacked. Stragglers – merchant ships that strayed from the main group – were easy targets for submarines.

A German U-boat

Torpedoes

ONLY ONE PERSON survived when a U-boat sank the Garsoppa *off Ireland in 1941.*

SAILING in convoy, the Empire Major *(above) collided with another ship.*

IN 1944 the Japanese submarine I-52 was sunk in the Atlantic, probably by depth charges from American planes.

SOUTH AMERICA

Straggler merchant ships were easy to attack

South Atlantic Ocean

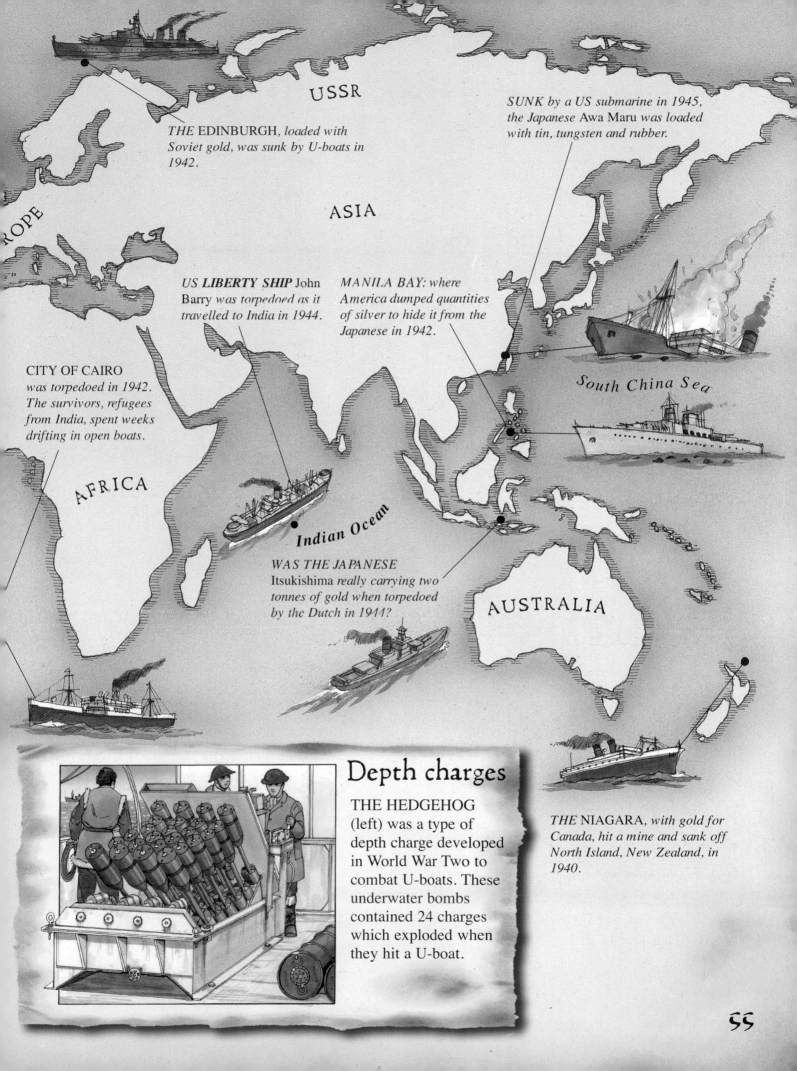

USSR

THE EDINBURGH, *loaded with Soviet gold, was sunk by U-boats in 1942.*

SUNK *by a US submarine in 1945, the Japanese Awa Maru was loaded with tin, tungsten and rubber.*

ASIA

US **LIBERTY SHIP** John Barry *was torpedoed as it travelled to India in 1944.*

MANILA BAY: *where America dumped quantities of silver to hide it from the Japanese in 1942.*

CITY OF CAIRO *was torpedoed in 1942. The survivors, refugees from India, spent weeks drifting in open boats.*

AFRICA

South China Sea

Indian Ocean

WAS THE JAPANESE Itsukishima *really carrying two tonnes of gold when torpedoed by the Dutch in 1944?*

AUSTRALIA

Depth charges

THE HEDGEHOG (left) was a type of depth charge developed in World War Two to combat U-boats. These underwater bombs contained 24 charges which exploded when they hit a U-boat.

THE NIAGARA, *with gold for Canada, hit a mine and sank off North Island, New Zealand, in 1940.*

ATTACK FROM THE AIR

U-boat quadruple anti-aircraft gun

IN WORLD WAR TWO ships faced attack from above and below. The aircraft and submarines used in World War Two were more sophisticated than those threatening ships in World War One. The **'ironclads'**, the great battleships that had dominated the earlier war, had been replaced by aircraft carriers – floating airfields that could take aircraft nearer their targets.

Air attack on a U-boat

Attack from below

LIKE ALL DEPTH CHARGES, the 'hedgehog' was a weapon designed for ships to use against U-boats in deep water. But it was soon adapted for shallow water, so planes could use it against U-boats near the surface.

Machine gun

A British submarine surfacing during a gale

Lookouts

THROUGHOUT World War Two, U-boats carried guns so that they could attack on the surface as well as underwater.

Japanese war planes attack Pearl Harbor, 1941

Pearl Harbor

ON 7 DECEMBER 1941, Japan attacked the US Pacific fleet at Pearl Harbor. The devastating attack made the US join World War Two. Just before 7.50am, 191 aircraft took off from six Japanese aircraft carriers and headed for Pearl Harbor. The USS *Arizona* (below) was one of the ships destroyed in the attack.

Sinking the *Bismarck*

18 MAY 1941: German battleship *Bismarck* sets out to attack Britain's Atlantic convoys. The British send cruisers *Norfolk* and *Suffolk* to shadow the *Bismarck*. The ships manoeuvre around each other in the north Atlantic. The *Bismarck* sinks the British ship *Hood*, but is itself hit three times, losing 1,000 tonnes of fuel.
26 May: Planes from the British aircraft carrier *Ark Royal* seriously damage the *Bismarck*'s rudder.
27 May: British battleships *Rodney* and *King George V* open fire with their big guns. Hit by one last torpedo, the *Bismarck* sinks – and 110 members of her crew are rescued.

The Arizona, *sunk in 1941*

The Bismarck

Swordfish bomber

SWORDFISH AIRCRAFT attacked the *Bismarck*, stopping it from threatening Allied ships.

MODERN DISASTERS

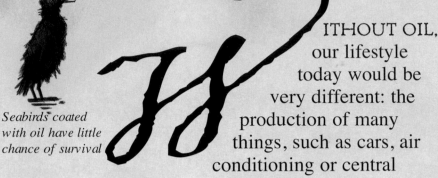

Seabirds coated with oil have little chance of survival

WITHOUT OIL, our lifestyle today would be very different: the production of many things, such as cars, air conditioning or central heating, gas or electricity, drugs and textiles, depends largely on oil. But oil must be transported from the producing countries, mostly in the Middle East, to other countries around the world. Supertankers holding over 400,000 tonnes transport oil across the earth's oceans. But the bigger the ship, the bigger the disaster if there is an accident.

Environmental damage

TODAY'S LARGE SHIPS need huge quantities of fuel. So when one runs aground and the fuel spills into the sea it does enormous damage. Fuel oil may be lighter than crude oil, but that's no help to dead seabirds or communities with beautiful beaches used by tourists.

Oil tanker Exxon Valdez

Oil pollution

IN MARCH 1989 the oil tanker *Exxon Valdez* ran aground in Prince William Sound in the Gulf of Alaska. It was an ecological disaster as 41 million litres of oil spilt from its tanks, polluting 1,930 kilometres of Alaska's coast.

American Star

In 1994, the *American Star* (left) ran aground off the coast of Fuerteventura. It was being towed to Thailand when its tow lines broke – it hit rocks and was split in two.

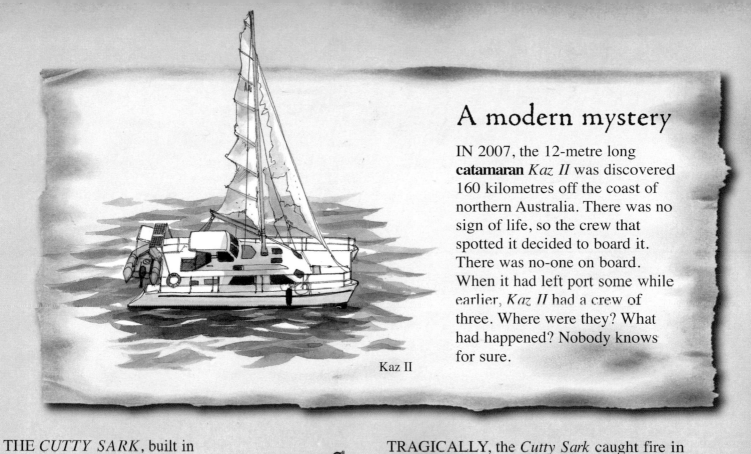

A modern mystery

IN 2007, the 12-metre long **catamaran** *Kaz II* was discovered 160 kilometres off the coast of northern Australia. There was no sign of life, so the crew that spotted it decided to board it. There was no-one on board. When it had left port some while earlier, *Kaz II* had a crew of three. Where were they? What had happened? Nobody knows for sure.

Kaz II

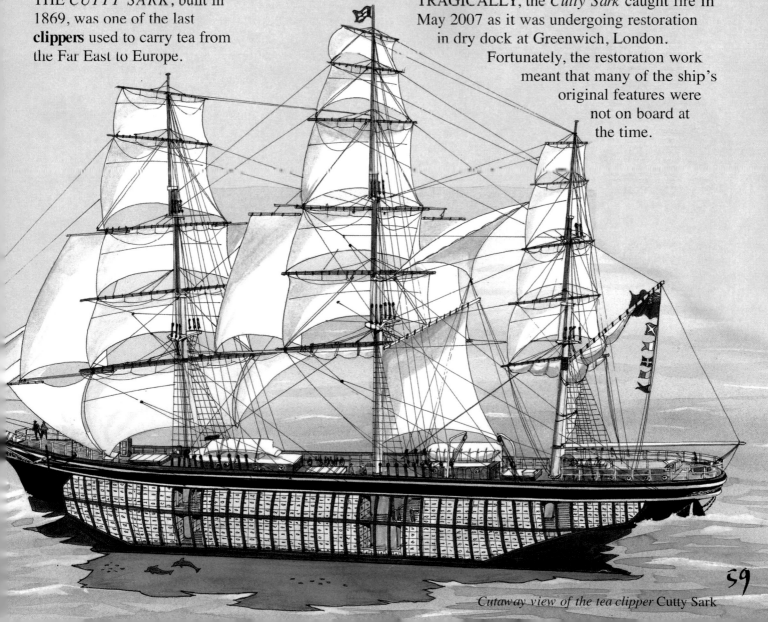

THE *CUTTY SARK*, built in 1869, was one of the last **clippers** used to carry tea from the Far East to Europe.

TRAGICALLY, the *Cutty Sark* caught fire in May 2007 as it was undergoing restoration in dry dock at Greenwich, London. Fortunately, the restoration work meant that many of the ship's original features were not on board at the time.

Cutaway view of the tea clipper Cutty Sark

FINDING WRECKS

BATHYSCAPHES (below) can dive deeper than any other sort of underwater craft. The crew's spherical compartment has walls of titanium or extra-thick steel to withstand the pressure in the deepest parts of the ocean.

Special ships take submersibles to their launch sites.

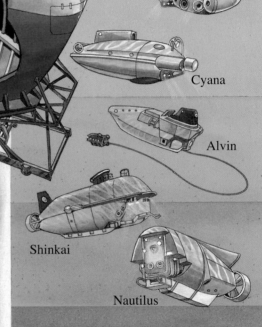

Diving saucer SP350

Cyana

Alvin

Shinkai

Nautilus

Titanium walls to withstand water pressure

Crew compartment

'Diving Saucer', 1959

LEGENDS ABOUT shipwrecks seem to suggest that every wrecked ship was loaded with treasure. Some were, some weren't. Finding wrecks depends on the technology available: the deeper a wreck, the longer it takes to find. (And raising them is another problem entirely!) Even wrecks that sank very publicly and close to shore, like the *Mary Rose* and the *Vasa*, get buried and can be lost for centuries. But the lure of finding treasure is as great as ever. And, of course, it depends how you define treasure! To archaeologists, those two ships, and the wrecks of ancient Greek and Roman ships in the Mediterranean, provide information more valuable than any gold or silver.

DIFFERENT SUBMERSIBLES are designed to dive to different depths. The greater the depth, the greater the problems faced by the engineers. In 1960 *Trieste FNRS III* descended 10,916 metres into the Mariana Trench, the deepest part of the Pacific Ocean, the earth's deepest ocean.

Trieste

Alvin

Exploring the deep

VESSELS THAT EXPLORE the deepest parts of the oceans can also be used to search for wrecks, especially those lying in very deep water. That was how *Titanic*'s wreck was discovered and explored in 1985. The robot *Jason Jr*, guided from the submersible *Alvin*, was able to go inside and explore the wreck.

Cable linking Jason Jr *to* Alvin

Jason Jr

Lights

Camera

Arm with gripper

61

GLOSSARY

Allies The group of countries that fought against Nazi Germany and other Axis countries during World War Two.

amphora a Roman wine jar.

astrolabe an instrument to calculate ships' latitude.

bathyscaphe a diving vessel used to reach the depths of the ocean.

bow the front of a ship.

bowsprit a large spar (pole) projecting beyond a ship's bow to help support the foremast.

carrack a large merchant ship of the 14th and 15th centuries.

catamaran a ship or boat with two linked hulls.

chart a sea map.

clipper a fast sailing ship.

colony a settlement in one country that is loyal to and obeys the laws of another country.

cross-staff a wooden instrument used to calculate a ship's position by measuring the position of the horizon and stars.

East Indiaman a big trading ship used by 18th-century East India Companies.

fire ship a ship set alight and sent into an enemy fleet in order to disperse the ships.

flagship the leading ship within a fleet.

forecastle a high platform at the bow of a ship used for fighting or accommodation.

frigate once a single-deck sailing warship; now a submarine hunter.

galleon a large 16th-century sailing ship.

galley a ship powered by oarsmen; also a ship's kitchen.

hull a ship's body and decks.

ironclad a 19th- or early 20th-century warship with an armour-plated hull.

keel a timber or steel beam along the base of a ship on which the framework is built.

knot the unit of measurement of a ship's speed.

Liberty ship a type of cargo ship built by the US during World War Two.

maiden voyage a ship or boat's first voyage.

piece of eight a valuable historic Spanish coin.

pirate a sea robber.

port the left-hand side of a ship.

privateer a sea robber licensed by a government.

ransom money demanded in exchange for the release of a prisoner.

rigging ropes that hold masts in place and control sails.

silt very fine soil deposited on the bottom of a sea or river.

sloop a small, fast sailing vessel, usually with one mast.

Spanish Armada the fleet sent by King Philip II of Spain to attack England in 1588.

starboard the right-hand side of a ship.

stern the back of a ship.

submersible a mini-submarine, launched at sea and recovered again by another vessel.

U-boat short for *Unterseeboot*, the German word for 'submarine'.

INDEX

INDEX

SHIP FACTS

End of an era At Tsushima, in 1905, the Japanese fleet heavily defeated the Russian fleet. This was the last battle to be fought by ships alone.

A terrible mess The worst ecological disaster caused by a ship was the oil spill from the *Exxon Valdez*. The supertanker ran aground off Alaska in 1988, flooding 1,930 kilometres of remote coastline with oil, and killing local wildlife.

Three times unlucky The *Hunley*, the first submarine to sink an enemy warship, sank three times before being lost to the sea for years. It was found and resurrected in 1995, and its final crew were buried with full military honours.

Out of your depth A submarine at a depth of 100 metres is totally unaffected by even the worst storm at the surface.

A one-way trip The Portuguese caravel *Vitoria* became the first ship to sail right around the world, in 1519–1521. Its captain was the explorer Ferdinand Magellan, but he did not live to complete the voyage. He was killed in the Pacific in 1520. After Magellan's death, the *Vitoria* was sailed home by one of his officers, Juan Sebastián del Cano.

Doomed relation-ship The Battle of Actium in Greece in 31 BC sank many ships – and led to a personal tragedy. At Actium, the Roman navy defeated a battle fleet belonging to Queen Cleopatra of Egypt and her lover, rebel Roman general Mark Antony. The Romans won, and Cleopatra killed herself rather than face capture by Rome.

Squeaky clean Guided-missile destroyers of the British Navy's 'Country' class (built 1963–1970) are completely washable. They have been designed so that every part of the ship can be washed down and decontaminated if they ever become polluted by radioactive fallout in a nuclear war.